RANGE WITHOUT MAN

THE NORTH FLINDERS

text—COLIN THIELE

photographs—MIKE McKELVEY

 RIGBY

ACKNOWLEDGMENTS

Grateful acknowledgment is made to Wallace
Stegner for the quotation from his book
The Sound of Mountain Water, and to
V. J. McLaglan for the quotation used on
pages 11–12. The quotation from Spot
Chadwick first appeared in the prose
works of W. J. Turner.

RIGBY LIMITED • ADELAIDE • SYDNEY
MELBOURNE • BRISBANE • PERTH

First published 1974
Copyright © 1974 Colin Thiele and Mike McKelvey
Library of Congress Catalog Card Number 73-75275
National Library of Australia Registry Card
Number & ISBN 0 85179 530 7

Wholly designed and set up in Australia
Printed in Hong Kong

Terrapinna Springs

—for spiritual renewal,
the recognition of identity,
the birth of awe—

"Save a piece of country like that intact, and it does
not matter in the slightest that only a few people every
year will go into it. That is precisely its value.
Roads would be a desecration, crowds would ruin it . . .

. . . We need to put into effect, for its preservation,
some other principle than the principles of exploitation
or usefulness or even recreation. We simply need that
wild country available to us, even if we never do more
than drive to its edge and look in. For it can be a
means of reassuring ourselves of our sanity as creatures,
a part of the geography of hope."

Wallace Stegner

RANGE WITHOUT MAN

It is more than mountain country, this wild land; more than a
tumultuous skyline in the blue distance or near-at-hand cliffs of
quartzite glowing like dragon's teeth. Much, much more. More even than
the gorges and harsh rock walls, the secret fissures, the knuckles and
knobs of ancient granite, the soft saltbush flats and grey plains between,
and the sudden unspeakable gift of water in rock-hole and creek.

It is solitude. For this is still in large measure the Range Without Man.
Go north from the Oratunga to Arcoona Bluff, north-east to Mount
Painter and the harsh tumult of the Gammons, on further still to
Mount Adams, Freeling Heights, and Mount Fitton until the ranges
dwindle away into low outriders like Mount Distance and Mount
Hopeless—and in all that vast tract of earth and sky, man is still the
least of things. Reduced in dimension. Taught humility.

From the highest points in the North Flinders, on days when the dust haze clears, it is possible to look out over the deeps of air into distance itself—far out west to the plains of Lake Torrens and the endless horizons of half a continent, and east likewise to the dry saltpans of Frome and Callabonna where the bones of ancient creatures lie held and hidden—history locked up in giant vats of salt. And everywhere there is that splendid solitude. Magnificent isolation.

It is still possible in this open and unpeopled region to feel the verities of silence and light, of star fall and eagle's flight, and to come to the brink of understanding. It is a place for poets, for painters—and, one hopes, for prophets. For wilderness there is, and hills enough for those who would lift up their eyes to them.

It is a region to be preserved at all costs, a place of inestimable value to the sanity of modern man. And yet, paradoxically, it needs protection from him, needs it desperately; needs bastions against the mindless, the vandalistic, the greedy, and the gauche. It needs far-sighted administrators, visionaries, and a race of teachers in the mould of Spot Chadwick who, in Melbourne nearly a century ago, taught lessons that rang in the minds of his students for a lifetime:

"You will find as you grow older, my dear fellows, that nothing is so beautiful as nothing or so permanently satisfying. This is because it may be everything, everything the heart has desired or the eyes have wished for; also because nothing is something you haven't got, and it is good, very good for the soul of man, not to have something . . . .

"Mark my words, some of you boys will live to see these unique regions . . . become the mere resorts of tourists, gridironed with macadamised roads over which will dash in thousands this disgusting new invention the motor car, which ten years ago crawled its filthy way along at fifteen miles an hour, was authorised last year in England to go at twenty miles an hour and will, I prophesy, very soon destroy space at the rate of a hundred miles an hour . . . .

"I tell you, boys, something has gone wrong with the mathematical god in charge of numbers; he has lost his memory or he has gone mad and suddenly changed his old unit of calculation for a new one, parsecs have taken the place of digits. All the beautiful bays and beaches of my boyhood are now turned into seaside cities black with people. The same is happening in every country. It will not be long before even Russia ceases to be a nation of peasants and forests and becomes industrialised like England, Germany, and the United States, all manu-facturing the same goods in astronomical quantities. The populations will become larger and larger and more standardised in order to consume them. Nobody sees the fatal writing announcing our doom or notices how rapidly the earth is shrinking to the size of a tennis ball. Long before some of you are dead it will be impossible to read on any map the words 'Desert,' 'Unknown Country,' 'Impenetrable Forest,' 'Waterless Region.' In the place of these names of hope and inspiration you will only be able to read: 'First-Class Hotel,' 'City Reservoir,' 'Electric Power Station,' 'Refuse Dump,' 'Crematorium,' 'Jewish Cemetery,' and 'Large Asylum for the Insane.' "

Spot Chadwick was remarkable not only because of the extra-ordinary accuracy of his classroom prophecies but because he was three generations before his time. He, perhaps alone among the teachers of his day, saw the value of wilderness to man, and recognised its attributes—waterlessness, inaccessibility, solitude—as things "of hope and inspiration."

The North Flinders would have pleased Chadwick. It can never be a place for half measures. It demands commitment. Harsh and barren in times of drought, glistening with summer heat, bitingly cold under winter wind or pre-dawn frost, its outlines for life are clear and bold. Here man's creature comforts are an anachronism, modern motels an incongruity. No place is closer to the great diurnal round of darkness and light, heat and cold—the certitude of earth's rhythms, the eccentricity and wonder of natural lore, of flood, drought, storm, calm, and famine.

Summer sunrise is a happening in brass and gold, like trumpets after silence. The morning comes up rapidly over the mountains in a high wide tide of light, sharpening, intensifying, until each rugged crest is etched in outline as bright as quicksilver. One feels the presence of the unseen sun. Light trembles on the brink. A moment longer it holds, the imminent rays shooting skywards, the air quivering with brightness. Then the first shafts blaze piercingly across the landscape, catching our eyes, exulting our spirits. Sunrise in the North Flinders is perhaps no richer in itself than in our otherwise daily lives, but there is a quality of newness here, a sense of the miraculous to set us trembling as if we were witness to the act of Creation.

The sharpness of morning light over these mountains and the flamboyance of sunset—colours that spread like flame in the cloud-banks, or fume and smoulder on the horizon as the west grows dark —are too rare and strange for cliché. As are the blue ridges at noon. But apart from everything that is huge—the immensity of distance and the rearing upthrust of mountainside and gorge—there is the minute and intimate: twig, bush and flower, reed and stem, pebble grain and

9

insect's wing. The infinite in the finite. One sees not only out and over, far and beyond, but near and closely, at and into. The colour of rock strata, the marks of mineralisation in chips of stone, the character of leaves and bark, all are part of this unique environment. And of its spirit.

Even vegetation is eccentric. Among the vertebrae of mountains, on the flats and plains between, there are open stretches of grass and bush, sometimes bordered by native pines—sombre trees with rough bark and clumps of orange lichens. There is a North American flavour about such scenes, a hint of northern Arizona. But then suddenly there are eucalypts to reassert Australia; a thundering gum in a watercourse or a spatter of slim-limbed mallee with bark hanging in long strips—whips, strops, flags of it, trailing and swinging in the wind. And on the plains, too, are acacia and bullock bush, bindi weed and cockspur, geranium creeper and wild spinach, and—where man hasn't destroyed it— saltbush and bluebush, and a scatter of different grasses: speargrass and button grass, seven day grass, river grass, and windmill grass.

For though one can still travel far without meeting man, his marks are there. Some of the signs are ancient—abandoned mines, derelict huts, crumbling walls, and bits of machinery littered about like frag- ments from a metal skeleton torn apart by dingoes. Here and there even a huge wheel intact, or a doorway and lintel, or an abandoned chimney stack in silhouette—the classic symbol of desertion. Almost all of them date from the 1860s and 1870s when copper, gold, lead, and silver were sought by a hardy breed of prospectors—Cornishmen mostly—who left their shafts and mullock heaps in the most inaccessible places. Gold at Bulyeroo, silver-lead at Silver Gap on Patsy Springs Station, copper at Mount Rose on Yankaninna and at a dozen places besides: Mount Serle, Balcanoona, Mount Freeling, Mount Burr, Sliding Rock, and the Mountain of Light. All gave promise and then retracted it, usually in the bankruptcy court.

More lasting consequences of man's incursion into the region stemmed not from his mining tools but from his animals. Goaded by an incredible conviction that "rain follows the plough," he actually settled the nearby plains for farming in the late 1860s. In his imagination places like Farina were to become bread bowls, the name itself typifying that hope. Today the flotsam of derelict cottages, the ribs of broken wheels, ruined tanks and wells, and other sad remnants are his monuments.

Unfortunately these attempts at agriculture and the development of pastoralism often did irreparable harm to the natural vegetation. Saltbush and bluebush were destroyed and in some areas have never regenerated. By 1870 all the land in the North Flinders had been leased for pastoral purposes and the flocks moved in. With them went the herdsman-shepherd, as ubiquitous as a shadow at a time when grazing was on the driven-herd principle and fences in the north were virtually unheard of. Overgrazing was almost inevitable, especially near the shepherd's hut and the main creeks and waterholes. Even today many of these spots are largely bare of growth, a terrifying illustration of man's lasting destruction of his environment.

Today the whole of the North Flinders and the plains on either side are "settled." Yet in all the country from Blinman to Moolawatana there are fewer than thirty stations. Many of the homesteads still shown on the maps are empty and abandoned, the occupants having moved out when the stations themselves ceased to exist as separate entities. This amalgamation and absorption of smaller properties into larger units illustrates the fact that small holdings are no longer economically viable. Survival by size seems to lie somewhere between an absolute minimum of a hundred square miles and the desirable dream of a thousand, although in a harsh world of high costs and low prices, of drought and loss, even size is no guarantee against disaster.

Rainfall is fickle. Stations such as Moolawatana on the plains at the edge of the Range hope to average five or six inches a year, but can go for years with virtually nothing; stations such as Yankaninna in the centre of the Range and at an average elevation of sixteen hundred feet count on seven or eight inches with some reliability. Paddocks are big— under forty square miles and many owners begin to feel a sense of constriction. But costs are big too. A thousand dollars a mile for dog-proof fencing, between two hundred and five hundred a mile for the rest, and there are hundreds of miles of fences on the bigger stations. Bores average upwards of five thousand dollars each, dams from ten to twenty thousand, transport thousands more.

Yet the actual work force is small. A few stations still employ permanent Aboriginal stockmen—and outstanding stockmen most of them have been—but the number could almost be counted on one's fingers. Even the total Aboriginal population is small, probably less than five hundred over the entire region. Many stations recruit labour seasonally, the one family virtually running things single-handed for the rest of the year, absorbing the disasters, making life-or-death decisions. It needs a special kind of man. "In all the stations of the northern Flinders," writes Vic McLaglan, "the most common factor is the type of men who own or manage these stations. Nearly all are men big and strong of body and ideals. They are Kiplingesque characters . . . who in times of adversity face problems so large and complex that the mind boggles. They are the end product of a process of natural selection." The inference is clear; in the North Flinders anything that is weak goes to the wall.

Unfortunately this harsh law of survival can also apply to things other than man—especially to fauna and flora under assault from without. A final legacy left by the miners of the last century was the goats they introduced for their own meat and milk and then allowed to run free. Today their descendants, like Biblical locusts, threaten the whole region. A quarter of a million are estimated to infest the northern section, and they are multiplying as prolifically as human beings.

Incredibly adaptable, the wild goat can survive climatic disasters that would leave other animals lying dead all over the landscape. Its digestive system can handle vegetation that its competitors must reject; it can climb to the most inaccessible places on cliffs or mountain tops and feed on the plant life there; it can even eat bark and samphire if it has to. Worst of all, in periods of drought it can climb trees and virtually live off the leaves—a devastating practice; especially for xerophytic species such as bullock bush and mallee which, having cast many of their leaves in the dry conditions, inevitably die when stripped of the rest.

As usual man, having introduced a pest without effort or thought, may find its eradication beyond his resources. Yet if he does nothing at all he may place much of the most beautiful part of the Flinders in jeopardy. Nor is it from goats alone that the threat to the ecological balance of the region comes. Rabbits, and overstocking with sheep and cattle, add to the danger. Men may once again find themselves more adept at creating deserts than they know.

This is not to say that nothing is being done anywhere. On some stations a deliberate policy of understocking, of developing carefully placed watering points, and of regenerating natural flora is showing the way to conservation and a controlled environment. But already much damage has been done, and correction will be a long process. In the end, however, one hopes that the spirit of the place is indestructible; that despite drought and erosion, pests, stock, and the hand of man, its uniqueness can remain for generations other than our own.

The sense of discovery recorded in the camp jottings of a recent diarist, reminiscent of what might have been written a century ago, does give cause for hope:

"7 June:
At Woodendinna Creek shallow ripple-stone ledges—water flows down slab bed. Cut across country from Narinna through highly mineralised country—copper stain very frequent, also heavy iron-stained rock with characteristic hollows and capsules. Terrain very weird—muted white, grey, green soil—tunnelling insect tracks making giant-sized "veins" raised above the soil's skin. Lots of ant lion nests. When down close to the ground everything looks in texture and colour like a moonscape . . . Cross country to Ben Lomond which lists to one side like a giant layer cake. Followed Chambers Creek through flood boulders and dense pines past Mount McFarlane. Chambers Creek is a natural line between the grass-covered open tableland on the west and the rugged pine hills of the east. Good grass, much wildlife—large flocks of pigeon, galah, corella, also wedge-tailed eagles, fork-tailed kite, emu, peregrine falcon, ringneck parrot. Camped late near Main Gap.

"8 June:
The country through Pinda Creek is heavily wooded with pines and mulga—the big gums stand out clearly from the scrubby pines. East from Christmas Mine are impressive quartzite cliffs and spectacular gorges.

"9 June:
Camped near the Angepena goldfields. Up early to shake the frost off the sleeping bags . . . Backtracked to Mount Hack—saw Warraweena Gap in the morning light, a formidable rock face looming out of the rolling hills of gums and pines. At Black Range Spring the country changed. Red bulldust gave way to hill after hill, mile after mile, of delicate lavender shale—such a subtle blending of pastel shades, with pale pines and gums accented by a white gum trunk or rough pine bark.

"11 June:
From Mulga View to Irish Well, then down to Moro Gorge, past flat squashed hills that look as if they've had a rake run over their spine— dry creek beds of dead trees. Reached Moro Gorge in late afternoon, an oasis of big gums with patinaed bark, and multitudes of birds. In the rock pools reeds and cat tails grow—some of the pools maybe nine or ten feet deep are lined with deep blue-green moss. Spot fairly accessible from the Wertaloona route so found the remains of previous campfires and way too many cans . . . .

"13 June:
Way to Yudaninna a seldom-used track leading across grassy plains with

large mobs of kangaroos. On our right the Gammon Ranges, rising red and rocky and forested with pine. After eight miles of bluebush and saltbush came to house at Yudaninna—not lived in now but must have been a pretty place with its view over a watercourse. Rough track to Illawartina Pound took us into the Gammons and good goat country. Climbed to the top of Benbonyathe Hill—could see almost all of the country we'd been through, including the Bunkers Ranges, and a lot we hadn't been to yet—full length of Lake Frome, Freeling Heights, Mount Painter, The Armchair, Mount Gee, etc.

'14 June:
Reclimbed Benbonyathe before sunrise—cold—photographed a fiery sun rising over Lake Frome, then walked down into Illawartina Pound. Rugged country. Goats very thick—saw mobs of forty to sixty animals scattered through the ridges.

'15 June:
As we ate our breakfast there was a noisy but pleasant commotion among the birds. Not only ringneck parrots, crows, galahs, a type of wattle bird, and wedge-tailed eagles way overhead, but also a mob of eight emus came to see us. They'd been attracted by our sleeping-bag sheet, airing in the breeze over a dead tree. Bump, bump, bump—they were the rudest-sounding of birds.

'17 June:
Sunrise at our camp at Moolawatana was spectacular as the low hills were lit orange before a cloud-darkened sky . . . After breakfast set out on the cross-country route to Lake Callabonna; reached it by noon and camped on the "shores." A narrow channel of water still remained but on the surface of the lake were skeletons of various birds perhaps caught in the muddy ooze before it dried . . . In other dry channels were cracked surfaces of mud flats forming abstract patterns of different coloured layers of mud. They crumbled beneath our feet or else gave way to a stinking black ooze sucking in everything touching its surface. Dead skeletons of twiggy bushes were draped with dried water moss, faintly resembling a surrealist stage setting. The entire lake (twenty miles across in spots) was unearthly, but the strangest things were camel tracks across the middle. They were from a mob of four or five who had crossed it at great speed many months before. Imagine *seeing* them lumbering across!
"The clouds overhead darkened and appeared threatening to our worrying eyes, but stationhands at Moolawatana had reassured us that no rain would fall for several months.

14

"After lunch decided to walk across lake to mound springs. Last November there was an eight-foot channel and twenty miles of water across the claypan. Picked out a spring mound on the opposite side and struck off. Magnificent desolation. On three sides of me the horizon floated on a mirage. Behind and to the west storm clouds pushed the sandhills into the lake. Underfoot the lake bed was a mosaic of unending variety. Large chips of sun-parched clay up to twenty inches across standing like sentinels on pedestals of black ooze. Sometimes small chips less than an inch in size scattered by the wind and curled into wind rows. Patches of dried water weed, small shells, yabbie holes. After about three miles the mirage faded out and the spring mould reconnected with the lake surface. Still a good mile away from the mound I found the carcass of a black swan. Closer to the spring were more carcasses, all juvenile birds not fully feathered and unable to fly. The spring mound was littered with hundreds of unhatched swan eggs. Counted sixty-two nests (intact, several broken nests); largest egg clutch was nineteen. Three adult bird carcasses, two on nest protecting eggs. Dingo and fox tracks abundant but apparently they had come after the birds were dead and the lake had dried up. No vandalism by foxes or dingoes but several eggs had been broken by ravens.

"One nest situated on edge of spring so close that bird could drink without getting up from incubating. Three springs functioning, largest one about two feet by four feet; water palatable. Half a dozen dead mulgas graced the leeward edge of the mound. Only other vegetation was low sedge and samphire.

"18 June:

Reached Mount Hopeless early morning. Could only locate it accurately by compass bearings. No wonder Eyre was disappointed when he got this far. As the northernmost point he reached, this low flat mesa rises unassumingly from a desolate plain . . . Rough gibber country—pebbles the size of oranges, gibbers the size of footballs. Eyre must have pulled his belt in a notch when he saw this from the top of the mesa . . . Many of map features are marked "P.D." (position doubtful). Examples are Mount Hopeless, Mulligan Hill, Mount Adams, Hamiltons Creek (upper reaches). They strike me as a minor understatement.

"19 June:

From our camp near Taylor Limestone Well we rose before sunrise to photograph the pastel-coloured lime hills. With the contrast of dark brown gibber against the chalky white, pink, and yellow of the washes, it reminded me of the Petrified Forest of Arizona. Only low sparse vegetation, some in pale pink flower. Sand in little arroyos was fine and white with little bird, reptile, roo, emu, and fox tracks. In the distance the not-so-rugged ranges reminded you that you were still in (or on the fringes of) the Flinders, but the stereotyped gum and red rock vistas were way behind you."

The virtue of the camp diary lies in its freshness and immediacy. This was the impact of the moment, and these were the ways of expressing it. And even though these quotations are no more than fragments from the whole they suggest the vastness of the region, its space and distance; and with it still a sense of excitement and discovery, a nearness to the elemental things that twentieth-century, mass-produced man is hungering for.

One need only see the rising flood of tourist advertising to read the ominous signs in such a hunger: "Escape must be offered from the fog and smog-bound cities of heavily industrialised Europe and North America, and their overcrowding. Pollution-cluttered rivers and lakes can be left behind for a while . . . The Flinders Ranges are a mecca for city dwellers in search of clear, sharp air . . . [Mountains] are arid, rugged and inhospitable, but to weary city dwellers of Europe, Japan, and North America they offer new life. They offer escape."

It seems so sad, like an echo. As if one has read it all somewhere before—in Switzerland perhaps, or Scandinavia, or Kenya, before these places were "discovered" as frontiers of nature. And the sadness deepens with more extracts from the same diary that come as unconscious postscripts to the advertisements: "Sign posts mark the way; lots of bottles and cans . . . Kleenex tissue and toilet paper outnumber the flowering plants." By contrast, at least, there is something hopeful and compelling in the picture of the same diarist preparing his first meal to come from a can on the sixth day out, then hammering the tin flat and placing the piece of metal back in his pack.

This, then, is the spirit of the North Flinders. A harsh, ancient landscape, certainly, but bold in its own strength and memorable in its loveliness. Wind and rain have been sculpting it for a million years since its primal forms were created, and the impassive cliffs and gorges seem constrained to endure a million more. Their sense of timelessness remains, symbolised by the wedge-tail in the high clear air above them. There is a touch of the infinite in his far height and the vastness of his gaze. A primeval solitude.

One hopes that for a moment longer this priceless region can remain the Range Without Man.

LIGHT AND SHADOW

Nothing accentuates the beauty of the Range more strongly than light and shadow. Sometimes it is a product of time or season, sometimes of aspect and location, often of all combined.

The early morning light literally runs full tilt from rock to rock on the crests of the ridges and pours uncontrollably down the broad slopes, lining in creek-beds and hollows with black shadow-like strokes of charcoal. Trees rear up hugely—sets on a vast stage with the floodlights on, theatre with gongs of brass and footprints of gold.

In the same way midday and evening have their scenarios too. Deep, narrow fissures stand in purple shade and twist into sudden sun; shadows plunge and lift; clefts and niches vary from minute to minute in gradations, tremors, echoes of light and shade. Rock-faces flare, stones stand up suddenly from the plains, limbs and leaves have silver outlines.

Sleep and waking, movement and rest, sound and silence are all surrounded by daylight's simple emphases, their rise and fall. Sunrise is a kind of festival; "let there be light" a daily commandment nobody can forget.

17

Above: Podocoma cuneifolia

Overleaf: Near Hodgson Hill

Facing page: Tributary to Chambers Gorge

Left: Brachina Gorge

Below: Tree and rock, Chambers Gorge

Right: Trunk of *Eucalyptus camaldulensis*

Overleaf: Overlooking Narrina Creek

23

WATERCOURSE, ROCK-POOL, AND TREE

In regions such as the North Flinders the supreme gift is water. Sometimes it lies curled in the channels and creek-beds, in long waterholes that are permanent even in times of drought; sometimes it hides secretly in tiny rock-holes and niches that must be discovered and cherished as they were by the Aborigines centuries ago. And rarely, when storms rage through the Ranges, the creeks and watercourses turn into instant rivers that roar down the gorges in flash floods, hurling aside gum trees and boulders, and scouring out channels, sweeping riotously down onto the plains, and dissipating their violence there in the vast distances of sand and sun and salt.

It was no coincidence that the early explorers followed the Ranges northwards. The creek-beds and pools were their tenuous life-lines, the permanent waterholes their bases for forward thrusts. And as the larger waterholes shrank into pools, the pools into soaks, and the soaks finally into barren clefts and hollows, so the impetus of the searchers faltered, and the place names on their maps changed from Lomond to Hopeless.

Even today, nothing delights the walker more fully than the unexpected discovery of a pool or spring in the Ranges, especially if the hollow is deep and the water clear. Sometimes there are even rushes and mosses, or the splash of a short stream over pebbles and ledges. But sweet water is usually elusive. Only the trees remain as signposts—leaves green, roots deep in crevice or fissure—symbolic of a union far more ancient than man.

Facing page: Yudanamutana Gorge

Brachina Creek

Left: Near Black Range Spring

Below and Right: Hamiltons Creek

THE LEAP OF COLOUR

The Flinders Ranges have always been synonymous with colour ever since travellers first stirred Sir Hans Heysen's imagination with stories of "the purple mountains" of the North. And Heysen himself led the nation to an awareness of that colour in his art, even though some of the early critics thought it harsh and unnatural. But Heysen even recorded its technicalities. "Up there you have to use something more like Prussian blue, an iron blue. It's harder, and the light plays on it. Actually the Prussian blue is not quite right either, so you have to experiment—use in addition a French ultramarine . . . And of course the red and yellow ochres . . . and the bronzes, you have to get the bronzes. Burnt sienna is an important colour too. Partly red."

It is good that a great painter set down the facts so clearly because even today there are still the unbelievers who say that such colours cannot exist. Yet they do. Distant blue at noon deeper than the blue-bag of grandma's wash, gnashing angry red on the cliffs, crimson in the west, hot, washed-out ochre and yellow, gentle mauve and violet in the shadows like fumes of evening smoke. They are all there. Sometimes from a sudden corner or cresting hilltop they burst on the traveller unbelievably, like a physical shock; sometimes they move and grow and fade slowly and distantly.

And close at hand the colours leap no less sharply. A band of rock, a stone, a thrusting outcrop—even orange lichen on bark. The walker in the Flinders has his day ringed with colour.

Upper Hamiltons Creek

Left: Mount Adams

Right: Ben Lomond

Below: Sunrise, Moolawatana

Overleaf: Upper Four Mile Creek

THE STERN ARIDITY

Beauty is not always comfort, nor water sweet gentleness. When the great salt lakes and claypans that hem in the North Flinders to east and west dry out, they shrink first into brackish flats and pools of brine, and finally harden into gleaming deserts of salt. Miraculously, sometimes, a mound spring pushes up drinkable water in the middle of it, but even here the earth is pitiless, and the summer ruthless. It is no place for the weak.

Beyond the lakes, beyond the outposts of the Ranges, are the gibbers and sand dunes and sad treeless wastes. Forlorn country, especially in times of drought. When Eyre stood on Mount Hopeless he named his standpoint well. Even within the Ranges, barrenness finds ways to show its teeth. Rock-strewn gullies stripped of growth, screens of stone, wind-swept dust, and the bare flanks of ridges give warning often enough. This country can be the Range without rain.

Near Taylor Limestone Well

Right: Gibber, Mount Hopeless

Left: Taylor Creek sunrise

Below: Taylor Creek sunset

Facing page, top: Upper Four Mile Creek

Mound Spring, Lake Callabonna

Facing page, bottom: Wirrapowie Creek

43

THE INTIMATE EYE

It is wrong to think of Australian landscape only in terms of the big distance or the bold outline. Inside each panorama there are a million littlenesses, often exquisite in their form and detail. This is certainly so in the North Flinders.

It is possible to look past the angry quartzite cliffs and the great granites of the Gammons to the track of a trilobite locked forever in stone, or the primeval cup of archaeocyatha, preserving its tiny clues to the dawn of life. If there are sermons in stone there are also lyrics, epigrams, and whispers.

The same is true of living flora and fauna. The intimate and searching eye will find miracles in a hundred places—the architectural precision of the wasp's mud nest, the loveliness of a native-pine cone, the tiny bark of a banded gecko, the fine design on the back of an inch-long skink.

And midway between the miniature and the grand there are filigrees of twigs and stems in tiny bushes, saplings like bonsai plants on the faces of the cliffs, and white tussocks in the dawn light growing from the rock.

In order to experience the kind of spiritual rebirth that wilderness regions can give, it is necessary to see with the intimate eye, to perceive what the poet Hopkins calls the "particularity of things." This is the perception that allows us to see "kingfishers catch fire, dragonflies draw flame;" the leap of the heart that springs from awareness and wonder.

Aristida sp.

Top left: Phyllurus milii, Barking Gecko

Top right: Aegotheles cristata, Owlet Nightjar

Left: Amphibolurus barbatus, Bearded Dragon

Below: Skin of *Tiliqua rugosa,* Sleepy Lizard

Facing page:

Top: Aboriginal rock carving, Olary Spur

Bottom left: Aboriginal rock carving, Red Canyon

Bottom right: Mud insect nest

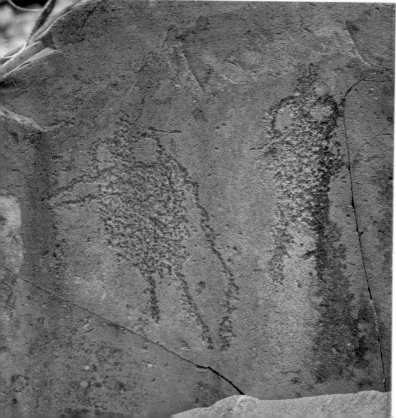

48

Left: *Sarcozena praecox*, Pigface

Centre: *Typha domingensis* at Morro Gorge

Below: *Enneapogon* sp.

Abandoned Black Swan nest, Lake Callabonna

Callitris, Native Pine

CLIFF-FACE, RIDGE, AND KNOB

Abrupt mountain walls belittle man's body and challenge his imagination. Most of us carry schoolroom pictures with us of Bass assaulting the faces of the Blue Mountains with crampons and grappling irons.

The cliffs of the Flinders are seldom a matter for climbers; there is no need. But they are a matter for photographers when the sun moves across the vertical and jagged sandstone or deepens the blue shadows of the gorges in sudden contrast. And certainly for poets, painters, and composers.

There are ridges, too, jumbled masses that rear into the sun and subside, grow steep or gentle, protrude or withdraw; and according to time, place, and season they give the Flinders the character that is uniquely theirs.

Sometimes humps and knobs of ancient rock bulge up and redden in the sun like inflamed excrescences on the bony plates of the Range; and single rocks as huge as houses, fashioned with a kind of wild geometry, lean out from the cliffs, their facets catching the light, their edges seemingly sharp enough to cut the shafts of sunshine. Wilderness such as this is neither uniform nor changeless; it is tumultuous and various.

The Needles, North Well Creek

Above: Near Mount Hack

Left: Mount Painter

Below: Upstream from Terrapinna Springs

Right: Acacia aneura

THE SOFTENED CONTOUR

The region of the Flinders Ranges is usually associated with sharpness of outline, angularity of form. Rocky aridity goes hand in hand with the hard edge—at least in the popular mind. And the association is accentuated by its traditional reputation for light and air: sharp, clear light that knows nothing of smog or pollution, and heaven-high steeps of dry sunny air—the tourist tout's bait to the "weary fog-bound hosts of the northern hemisphere."

But there is also much that is gentle and mellow. Distant arenas, amphitheatres, hollows in the hills are often softened and rounded; eroded foothills at the base of the main ranges are smoothed by erosion into humps and knolls as curved as nude breasts, and sometimes the long slopes fall away to the plains as gently as they do in the undulating pasture lands of the south.

Plant life adds to the softened contours. Bushes and trees give fluidity to the landscape, and tussocks hide sharp edges. Cloud shadows move across the Ranges too, camouflaging the scarps and darkening the valleys. On some days a visitor could come away convinced that this was a gentle region.

Xanthorrhoea quadrangulata at Olary Spur

Overleaf: Wilkawillina Gorge

Facing page, left: Woodendinna Creek

Left: A.B.C. Range

Below: Mount McKinlay

Overleaf: Mount McCallum

Arid woodland, Upper Chambers Creek

Gammon Ranges

THE RESIDUES OF MAN

The signs of man's comings and goings are to be found everywhere in the Ranges. First and infinitely foremost, the marks of the Aborigines still remain despite time and weather and the ravages of white vandals. If the most precious of the paintings can be kept secret and hidden from the crass and the insensitive, there may be hope yet for their preservation. For the Aborigines themselves have dwindled or dispersed until even they have lost the significance of the artist's purpose or the location of the sacred places.

A hundred years of the white man's passage are mapped out everywhere too. Stone wall, derelict chimney, broken wheel, rusting metal, and mounds of mine-shaft mullock are scattered through the Ranges like litter. But in most cases the action of wind and rain, and the regeneration of natural growth, has begun to soften the scars and hide the debris.

In the end, therefore, we come back to the relationship between man and Wilderness. The weals he has left in the Flinders, small though his numbers were, and the long slow process of recovery still going on, are pointers enough to the uneasiness of that relationship.

Aboriginal rock carving

"Cadnia East"

Stone wall, Mount Lyndhurst

Aboriginal ochre paintings

Facing page: Along Hamiltons Creek

"Old Illinawortina"

"Old Illinawortina"